IMPROMPTUS

IMPROMPTUS

SELECTED POEMS

GOTTFRIED BENN

edited and translated by

MICHAEL HOFMANN

FABER & FABER

First published in the USA in 2013
by Farrar, Straus and Giroux
First published in Great Britain in 2014
by Faber and Faber Ltd
Bloomsbury House,
74–77 Great Russell Street,
London WC1B 3DA

Typeset by RefineCatch Limited
Printed in England by T. J. International Limited, Padstow, Cornwall

Statische Gedichte. Edited by Paul Raabe © 1948, 2006
by Arche Literatur Verlag AG, Zürich-Hamburg

Sämtliche Werke copyright © 1986, 1987, 1989, 1991
Klett-Cotta—J. G. Cotta'sche Buchlandlung Nachfolger GmbH, Stuttgart

Introduction, selection and translation © Michael Hofmann, 2014

The right of Michael Hofmann to be identified as translator of
this work has been asserted in accordance with Section 77
of the Copyright, Designs and Patents Act 1988

A CIP record for this book
is available from the British Library

ISBN 978–0–571–28926–4

FSC
www.fsc.org
MIX
Paper from
responsible sources
FSC® C101712

2 4 6 8 10 9 7 5 3 1

for Christian Wiman and Don Share
and for Alan Jenkins and the late Mick Imlah

THANKS AND ACKNOWLEDGEMENTS

I owe thanks, once again, to Jonathan Galassi for the trust – impulsive to begin with, then steady and unfazed – which he brought to this project. From the moment I first took it to him in 2005, he contrived to give me the feeling that whatever I came up with (and wherever and whenever), he would be ready for it: an extraordinary sense to get from a publisher.

One of the pleasant aspects of something long-running as this has been is it gives one a dependable subject of conversation with friends; Jonathan Aaron, Durs Grünbein, Lawrence Joseph, Paul Keegan, and Jamie McKendrick were all good enough to bandy Benn with me for many hours.

The manuscript has benefited from thoughtful and lynx-eyed readers in Mareike Grover, Chris Richards, Miranda Popkey and Martha Sprackland.

Extravagant thanks – really *outré* thanks – to the princes who edit *Poetry* (Chicago) and the *Times Literary Supplement* for giving Benn house-room ('a house is not an inn') in their journals. The book is dedicated to them.

Some of these poems first appeared in the following places, sometimes in (something I've wanted to say for years!) slightly different versions: *The Faber Book of 20th-Century German Poems*; *Little Star*; *The New Republic*; *The New York Review of Books*; *The Paris Review*; *Poetry*; *The Poetry Book Society Anthology No. 3* (1992); *The Times Literary Supplement*.

CONTENTS

Though Gottfried Benn can scarcely be said to exist in the English-speaking world, there are a surprising number of prominent mentions of him. T. S. Eliot for instance, in his essay 'The Three Voices of Poetry' goes so far as to associate one such voice – the first, 'the voice of the poet talking to himself – or to nobody' – with Benn. John Berryman allows him the end of one Dream Song, no. 53: 'and Gottfried Benn / said: – we are using our own skins for wallpaper and we cannot win.' In his novel *Plexus* Henry Miller is careful to leave the 1927 issue of Eugene Jolas' avant-garde magazine, *transitions*, lying around, and quotes *in extenso* from Benn's essay in it. Frank O'Hara has a tilt at him in one of his invariably disastrous and perplexing diatribes, when he seems to have his ill-fitting Hector the Lecturer suit on: 'Poetry is not instruments / that work at times / then walk out on you / laugh at you old / get drunk on you young / poetry's part of your self.' ('To Gottfried Benn')

With all these appearances, you would have thought Benn had to have some being somewhere. But it's more like that space radiation called 'chatter'; there's something that leads our instruments to think there's something 'out there'; we might even give it a name, but most of us remain doubtful, and few of us expect ever to see it. I don't think you could fill a room with a conversation about Benn – non-Germans and non-Germanists, that is. And yet we're talking of someone of the eminence, say, of Wallace Stevens, someone most Germans (and most German poets, too) would concede as the greatest German poet since Rilke.

Basically, Benn has appeared once in English, namely in E. B. Ashton's book, *Primal Vision*, first published in 1958, and still in print with Marion Boyars. The trouble with Ashton's book – and in this it perhaps betrays its origins in the post-War decade – is that it is not primarily interested in Benn the poet, but the man of ideas, the German, and the 'pheno-type'. One has to wonder at the judgement and effectiveness (not to mention the long monopoly) of a book introducing a foreign poet to an English readership that is three parts prose, and where the translations of the poems (one eighth of the whole) are starchy, cumbrous and muted. They have neither the attack nor the ease of Benn in German – to me he is both the hardest and the softest poet who ever lived. Thus unsuc-cessfully transmitted, Benn has no English admirers; unlike Brecht, he's not even unpopular. It's only stray foreign readers, like Joseph Brodsky or Adam Zagajewski, who read him in a third or fourth language, or in the original, who have anything like a true or a full sense of Benn.

*

Benn called his autobiography *Doppelleben*, but for once (see 'St Petersburg – Mid-Century', see 'Bauxite', see 'Fragments, 1955') he perhaps wasn't interested in counting, because I can see more like four of him: the military man, the doctor, the poet and the ladies' man. With their different rhythms and urgencies and tolerances, these four identities – four suits of cards, two black, two red, two professional alibis, two pas-sions, two kinds of truancy and two kinds of work – shaped and complicated his life. He ran from woman to woman, but also from woman to poem, from poem to uniform, from uni-form to lab coat, and back again, and with all the possible variations. Style trumps facts, he said, and good stage-management trumps fidelity. But within the constraints of his circumstances and especially his tightly drawn financial limits (very rarely in his life did he have money), he was at pains to be a gentleman (it's not a word one hears often nowadays, but it's a concept he certainly understood and tried to live by) and to lead an upright life: that is, one informed by distance and warmth and good presentation. Accordingly, the most important and longest-lasting relationship of his life was conducted largely by mail over twenty-four years with the Bremen businessman F. W. Oelze. Benn aspired – or resigned himself – to be at once an earl and a pariah. He was a brilliant and internationally acclaimed writer of poetry and prose, who never came close to being able to live by it; a notably unenthusiastic doctor, who nevertheless helped his 'Schmutzfinke von Patienten' (his 'squalid patients') as much as he could; an amorous and courtly man and an inveterate buyer of flowers for his wives and mistresses and casual liaisons; by his left eye he had the Mensur, the German duelling-scar, and twice in his life – during the two world wars – he fell back into the army, where, ironically, he enjoyed the periods of greatest peace and productive contentment in his life.

*

Benn's first publication in 1912 – a small-press pamphlet called Morgue and Other Poems, one of the great debuts in literary history – catches him at a typical juncture: he had recently qualified as a medical doctor in Berlin; he was having an affair with the Jewish German poet and free spirit Else Lasker-Schüler; and he was – if the reader will allow the expression, it's still more accurate than any other I can think of – moonlighting with the army, which had paid for his education. When the First World War broke out, Benn – like so many others – quickly got hitched (though not to Lasker-Schüler), conceived a daughter (Nele was born in September, 1915), and joined up again. For three years he was behind the lines in Brussels, as a 'doctor in a whorehouse'; it was one of those immensely suggestive, paradigmatic times in his life when he was at once becalmed, isolated and productive; the nation was distracted and engorged, but Benn was reading and writing. He writes about it with grateful rapture, almost as though he

[xiii]

were a Medieval monk left to illuminate manuscripts behind stone walls a yard thick. After the war, he tried to find the same seclusion as a skin doctor and venereologist, in private practice in Berlin, but that quality of '*béguinage*' (his word – a religious seclusion) remained something best provided by the army. Accordingly, in 1935, he tried the same thing again: left Berlin, re-enlisted, and (in 1938) re-married. In World War Two he fetched up at the fortress town of Landsberg an der Warthe (today the Polish town of Gorzow Wielkopolski), which he commemorated contemporaneously in the prose of *Block II, Room 66* ('Nothing so dreamy as barracks!') – where, under-employed by the army, as the senior medical man with the rank of colonel, he wrote, while waiting for the German defeat, poems, essays, and prose – among them many pieces that would certainly have cost him his liberty and most probably his life if they had been turned over to the SS.

A brief note on the vexed and controversial circumstances that restored him to the bosom of the army. Almost all his life, Benn had no expectations of governments (it's hard to imagine him voting, impossible to guess which way); human existence was futile, progress a delusion, history a bloody mess, and the only stay against fatuity was art, was poetry. Writing should have no truck with any social or political aims. Anything less like the useful, obedient and subsidised creature the 'state poet' than Gottfried Benn is impossible to imagine. Then, in 1933 and 1934, Benn drifted into the Nazi orbit. For a brief while it looked to him as though his long-range ideas about the human species, his cultural pessimism, his Nietzschean and Spenglerian gloom had somewhere to dock. He drafted the declaration of loyalty to the newly returned Nazi government that precipitated mass resignations from the *Preussische Akademie der Künste*, to which he had only recently been elected; he addressed a sharp 'reply to the literary émigrés' to (his adoring admirer) Klaus Mann; he gave a talk welcoming the Italian Futurist (and Fascist) poet F. T. Marinetti to Berlin; he was briefly Vice-President of Hitler's *'Union Nationaler Schriftsteller'*. Mutual disenchantment was not slow in coming; the relationship's fleeting appearance of compatibility shaded into, or gave way to its natural level of implacable – and for Benn, extremely threatening – mutual detestation. It dawned on Benn that the Nazis were not a bunch of pessimistic aesthetes like himself, but rather imbued with a sanguinary optimism; by the time of the Night of the Long Knives in June, 1934, he was fully disabused. They, meanwhile, never forgave him for his early writings and his Jewish associations, got him struck off the medical register as a suspected Jew (Benn=Ben!), and banned him from writing altogether in 1938. They could hardly fail to find his work 'degenerate', as they did that of his Expressionist colleagues in the visual arts. At this point, Benn left Berlin and took refuge in the army, which in a typically stylish and abrasive phrase he described as 'the aristocratic form of emigration.' He wrote an analysis on suicides in the military. All this feels to me known or partly known, understood or partly understood, in the English-speaking world. It remains an anomalous and troubling interval in his life, before, so to speak, normal disservice was resumed; to use it as grounds for not reading Benn – to play the 'Fascist card' – is merely lazy and a little hysterical. Few of the Modernists, after all, had the credentials of good democrats.

Most everything else in his life comes under the heading of *'Herkunft, Lebenslauf – Unsinn!'* ('background, CV – tosh!'), as he inimitably and contemptuously put it. Still, in the wake and a little in the manner of his contempt, here goes: father a clergyman, mother originally in service, from the French-speaking part of Switzerland. (In his dry, geneticist way, Benn makes as much of his mixed parentage as, say, Thomas Mann.) Born in one vicarage, grew up in another. The second of eight children, and the oldest son. Sent away to school at the age of ten. He studied religion at the behest of his father, before being allowed to switch to literature and medicine. In 1914, he was a ship's doctor on a trans-Atlantic steamship; he liked to claim he was so hard up he couldn't even afford to get off and tour New York. He was the doctor, in 1916, officiating at the execution by a German firing squad of the British nurse Edith Cavell and her Belgian helper, who had been found guilty of treason. The year 1922 saw the death of his mother from untreated breast cancer (see 'Jena') and his first wife, Edith Osterloh from a botched appendectomy (the fact that he and Osterloh had lived separate lives didn't keep Benn from being deeply affected by her death); incompetent or at least unambitious in most practical matters, he arranged to have Nele adopted by a Danish couple; toward the end of his life, he painstakingly rebuilt a relationship with her. In 1938, he married his second wife, Herta von Wedemeyer. Amid the confusion of the ending war, in July 1945, sent away by him to the west for her own safety, she committed suicide, convinced she would fall into the hands of the Russians. Surely the poem 'Death of Orpheus' owes something to her harrowing circumstances, and his grief and guilt. Following the defeat, occupation and then partition of Germany, Benn returned to West Berlin, opened another practice, and married a third time: Ilse Kaul, a dentist. Because of his sometime pro-Nazi positions, he wasn't allowed to publish by the Allies: 'undesirable then,' he wrote, a little smugly, 'undesirable again now'. The Swiss publisher, Arche, brought out *Static Poems* in 1948, ushering in a great wave of Benn's late work. He was awarded the Büchner Prize in 1951. In May 1956, his seventieth birthday was celebrated with the publication of a *Collected Poems*, beginning with the recently composed 'Can Be No Sorrow'. On 7 July 1956, at a time when the earth would indeed 'yield[s] easily to the spade,' Gottfried Benn died in Berlin.

*

Benn's name is indissolubly connected to the German, or perhaps Nordic, movement of Expressionism, like its direct contemporaries Imagism or Dadaism, a proto-modern movement, but fiercer than the one, and less theatrical than the other. Literary Expressionism has almost as many meanings as it has practitioners, but in a general way (and certainly in Benn) I think of it as a simultaneous boosting of both style and content. Expressionism is gaudy, neo-primitive, volatile, provocative, anti-rational. The brain is eclipsed by its older neighbours: the glands, the senses (including the oldest sense, the sense of smell). Expressionism is momentary, it doesn't count days or verify destinations. It might be the humdrum Baltic – shallowest and newest and saltiest of seas, sea-beach to Berlin – but it feels like the Aegean, if not the South Pacific, in the poet's rhapsodic imagination. Expressionism hymns a simpler physis, the body under its own management. Down with the boardroom, away with the little pin-striped simpleton or puritan upstairs! Expressionism is an as-if, or an if only: if only the body could write or paint or think! Or not-think. Poems like 'Express Train' or 'Caryatid' or 'Asters' are literary equivalents to the brash, paradisiac canvases of Emil Nolde or Ernst Ludwig Kirchner or Ferdinand Hodler.

Benn's very first poems were off-cuts of *materia medica*: *Morgue* and *Fleisch* were among his titles, a prose book was called *Gehirne* (brains). As with a lot of Expressionist writing, it was hard to see how it might develop, not least because it was all already so fully and shockingly *there*: brash, confrontational, destructive, appalling. Benn wasn't sure either. In a splendidly saturnine note in his first *Collected Works* of 1921 (he was 35), he wrote: 'Now these complete works, one volume, two hundred pages, thin stuff, one would be ashamed if one were still alive. No document worthy the name; I would be astonished if anyone were to read them; to me they are already very distant, I toss them behind me like Deucalion his stones; maybe human beings will emerge from the gargoyles; but whether they do or not, I shan't love them.' I don't know that I have ever seen anything less self-enamoured, less *parti pris* from a poet on his/her own work! In the event, something of what he so indifferently predicted did come to pass: 'human beings' did emerge from the 'gargoyles' – whether or not Benn loved them hardly matters. His later poems lost their ferocity, their shock, and their prankish, metallic manipulativeness; became softer, lived-in, improvised, gestured-at, shuffling or shambling. They still had the same principal two ingredients: corpses – or mortality – and flowers; the same groping at one notion or another of a 'beautiful youth.' The 'lavender asters' return in the form of new flower-complexes, as 'lilacs [. . .] narcissus colour, and smelling strongly of death,' as poppies, phlox, gladioli, the 'old and reliable ranunculi of Ostade', hydrangeas, and finally as forsythias and lilacs again, this time 'with hope of roses'. The beautiful or unbeautiful, loved or unloved cadavers have turned into Benn himself, anxiously remembering the ghosts of his salad days; or hoping to hold on, into June (of the year of his death – he died on 7 July); or in one of his last poems (the first one here, 'Can Be No Sorrow'), thinking soberly and unflinchingly about the deaths of poets, put together from wood and tears and pain and spasm, the 'sleep well' at once a close echo and a world away from the cynical 'rest easy' of 'Morgue'.

During the 1920s and '30s, Benn found a way of parlaying his short, explosive free verse poems into lengthier, internal combustion pieces. His characteristic form became the tightly rhymed octave, often in very short two or three foot lines. The longings and strictures and surfeits articulated in these are often very beautiful and bizarre, but barely translatable, not even when there are equivalents – perhaps especially not when there are equivalents. Or what is the English, pray, for: '*Banane, yes, Banane / vie méditerranée*'? 'Banana, yes, banana / Mediterranean life?' I don't think so. A blizzard of neologisms, incantatory and highly personal charm-words, flower-names and technical terms; sociopathic hatred; a texture of fierce and luxurious depression. Benn pines for 'Mediterranean,' 'Palau', 'Night', 'Cocaine', 'Anaesthesia'. Life is '*niederer Wahn*', lower or lesser madness, in its place Benn calls for '*thalassale Regression*', for form, trance, elevation. It might seem Decadent, 1890s-ish, only there is no pose about it, nothing effete. For all the Verlaine-like sonorities of the poems, there are ferocious energies at work within them. I am conscious that the poems of this period are under-represented here. I'm afraid they were too difficult and idiosyncratic for me to carry them into English in any important way. I preferred to go, more or less straight, from the shocking early to the weary late: to those beerily misanthropic and magically beautiful mutterings of Benn's last two decades that have always particularly entranced me as a reader. Two world wars, two marriages, two bereavements, careers in the military and medicine, and forty years of writing, have gone into their making. '*Ausdruck und Stoffvernichtung*', 'expressiveness and destruction of subject-matter' they are. They come with their own silence and space. Like the early poems, they are as they are, are as they want to be. The opposite of art, Benn always argued, is not actually nature, but a desire to please.

Thus, the hardness of the early style – the 'gargoyles' – is replaced by human tenderness, empathy, puzzlement, a kind of unfocused but unavoidable sadness. The 'young jackal,' he sweetly suggests in an essay somewhere, has indeed turned into 'an old gazelle.' It is as though the poems themselves – and this strikes me as extremely rare in poetry, Eugenio Montale's late, *retrobottega* poems a further instance – *are old*; have undergone an aging process, cellular and organic, like flesh; their resources – a mild, as it were stoical, plaintiveness, a burbling, flaccid syntax, an unsolicited melancholy, a

[xix]

heaping of negatives – are those of age; breathing and humming and carpet slippers and *Juno* cigarettes and murmuring
and pain and a human smell have gone into them – not mere,
dime-a-dozen words. At bottom, life is unchanged in thousands
of years: still solitude, still doubt, still want of recognition;
poetry is always questioning and at odds with life; always
'the insufferable / difficulties of outward-directed expression.'
You see the jowly man in front of his chaotic shelves. That
'fascination' that Benn identified as the elusive but irreducible
quality of poetry inheres in them as much as it does in the
rhyming strophes; effectively, both are collages of the most
varied and spirited diction. The growly misanthropic cuss who
speaks them is as much an invention and a function of style as
the brittle and glitteringly impersonal manner of the octaves.
Though light as lace, they are wonderfully heavy with
experience, 'a pile of life in variegated forms'.

Yeats says the poet 'is never the bundle of accident and
incoherence that sits down to breakfast; he has been reborn
as an idea, something intended, complete.' Really not so
Benn, not in these last poems. He is absolutely the bundle
seated – if not to breakfast exactly, then at least in the corner
of the bar after work in the evening, downs two or three
beers, smokes his *Junos*, listens to the radio, listens to the
chatter of the other customers, scribbles something trenchant-
ly doleful on a pad. It is rare for art to be so perspicuous, to be
made from so extravagantly little – sometimes just 'a dish / of
sausage soup, (free on Thursdays / with a beverage)' – so to
pair grace with dailiness, discretion with intimacy, a shy
wistfulness with stoicism.

Somehow, quite without my realising it, I have spent half my
life with Benn; back in his centenary year, 1986, I reviewed the
two-volume edition of his poems and Holthusen's begun
biography of him. He has influenced me, not only *to* translate
him in the first place, but also *while* translating him. Over the

years, thanks in part to Benn, my own sentences have become more indeterminate, my language more musical, my diction more – no pun intended – florid. There is a sort of murmurous, *mi-voix*, *halblaut* quality in poems that I adore, and – languidly – strive for. I was all the time quietly being readied for a task I hardly dared suppose I would ever take on. I loved these poems when I first read and wrote about them half a lifetime ago; somehow – youth? trepidation? selfish possession rather than working to make them available to an English readership? – I never allowed myself to think I might actually translate them.

MICHAEL HOFMANN

Can Be No Sorrow

That narrow cot, hardly any bigger than a child's, is where
    Droste-Hülshoff died
(it's there in her museum in Meersburg),
on that sofa Hölderlin in his tower room at the carpenter's,
Rilke and George in hospital beds, presumably, in
    Switzerland,
in Weimar, Nietzsche's great black eyes
rested on white pillows
till they looked their last –
all of it junk now, or no longer extant,
unattributable, anonymous
in its insentient and continual disintegration.

We bear within us the seeds of all the gods,
the gene of death and the gene of love –
who separated them, the words and the things,
who blended them, the torments and the place where they
    come to an end,
the few laths and the floods of tears,
home for a few wretched hours.

Can be no sorrow. Too distant, too remote,
bed and tears too impalpable,
no No, no Yes,
birth and bodily pain and faith
an undefinable surge, a lurch,
an unearthly stirring in sleep
moved bed and tears –
sleep well!

6 January 1956

1912–1920

Little Aster

A drowned drayman was hoisted on to the slab.
Someone had jammed a lavender aster
between his teeth.
As I made the incision up from the chest
with the long blade
under the skin
to cut out tongue and palate,
I must have nudged it because it slipped
into the brain lying adjacent.
I packed it into the thorax
with the excelsior
when he was sewn up.
Drink your fill in your vase!
Rest easy,
little aster!

Beautiful Youth

The mouth of the girl who had lain long in the rushes
looked so nibbled.
When they opened her chest, her oesophagus was so holey.
Finally in a bower under the diaphragm
they found a nest of young rats.
One little thing lay dead.
The others were living off kidneys and liver
drinking the cold blood
and had had themselves a beautiful youth.
And just as beautiful was their death, and quick:
the lot of them were thrown into the water.
Ah, will you hearken at the little muzzles' oinks!

Circulation

The solitary molar of a streetwalker
whose body had gone unclaimed
had a gold filling.
All the rest were gone,
as if by tacit agreement.
This one the morgue attendant bagged for himself,
flogged it, and had himself a night out on the proceeds.
Because, so he said,
only clay should revert to clay.

Night Café

824: Lives and Loves of Women.
The cello takes a quick drink. The flute
Belches expansively for three beats: good old dinner.
The timpani has one eye on his thriller.

Mossed teeth in pimple face
Waves to incipient stye.

Greasy hair
Talks to open mouth with adenoids
Faith Love Hope round her neck.

Young goitre has a crush on saddle nose.
He treats her to onetwothreee beers.

Sycosis brings carnations
To melt the heart of double chin.

B flat minor: the 35th Sonata.
Two eyes yell:
Stop hosing the blood of Chopin round the room
For that rabble to slosh around in!
Enough! Hey, Gigi! –

The door melts away: a woman.
Dry desert. Canaanite tan.
Chaste. Concavities. A scent accompanies her,
                              less a scent
Than a sweet pressure of the air
Against my brain.

An obesity waddles after.

[8]

Alaska

Europe, Europe's just a bogey in a confirmand's nose,
We're going to Alaska!

Ocean man, jungle man,
Gives birth to everything out of his belly,
Eats seal, shoots bear, from time to time
Shoves something up a woman:
A man.

The Young Hebbel

You carve and sculpt, the deft chisel
in a soft shapely hand.
I beat my head against the marble
to knock it into shape,
my hands work for a living.

I am still a long way from myself,
but I want to become Me!
There is someone deep in my blood
who cries out for home made
Olympuses and worlds for humans.

My mother is such a poor wretch,
you'd laugh if you saw her,
we live in a tight annex,
built onto the end of the village.
My youth is like a scab:
under it there is a wound
that every day leaks blood.
It disfigures me.

I don't need sleep,
food just enough to keep from starving.
An implacable struggle
and the world bristling with sword points.
Each one hungers for my heart.
Each one, I, unarmed,
must melt in my blood.

Threat

Know this:
I live beast days. I am a water hour.
At night my eyelids droop like forest and sky.
My love knows few words:
I like it in your blood.

Songs

I

O that we might be our ancestors' ancestors.
A clump of slime in a warm bog.
Life and death, fertilising and giving birth
Would all be functions of our silent juices.

An algal leaf or a sand dune,
Shaped by the wind and basal and heavy-set.
Even a dragonfly's head or a gull's wing
Would be too evolved and suffer too much.

Contemptible are the lovers, the mockers,
All despair, yearning, and hope.
We are such painfully plague-ridden gods,
And yet we think continually of God.

The soft bay. The dark forest dreams.
The stars, snowball-blossom big and heavy.
Panthers lope silently among the trees.
Everything is strand. Forever calls the sea –

Then Icarus fell at our feet,

Cried: Boys and girls, multiply!
Get into that poorly ventilated Thermopylae! –
He tossed one of his thighs at us,
Flipped over, and was finished.

Express Train

Brown. Brandy-brown. Leaf-brown. Russet.
      Malayan yellow.
Express train Berlin–Trelleborg and the Baltic resorts.

Flesh that went naked.
Tanned unto the mouth by the sea.
Deeply ripened for Grecian joys.
How far along the summer, in sickle-submissiveness!
Penultimate day of the ninth month!

Athirst with stubble and last corn-shocks.
Unfurlings, blood, fatigue,
Deranged by dahlia-nearness.

Man-brown jumps on woman-brown.

A woman is something for a night.
And if you enjoyed it, then the next one too!
Oh! And then the return to one's own care.
The not-speaking! The urges!

A woman is something with a smell.
Ineffable! To die for! Mignonette.
Shepherd, sea, and South.
On every declivity a bliss.

Woman-brown drapes itself on man-brown:

Hold me! I'm falling!
My neck is so weary.
Oh, the sweet last
Fevered scent from the gardens.

Englisches Café

The whole soft-shoe gaggle
Of Russians, Jewesses, dead peoples, distant coasts,
Slinks through the spring night.

The violins green. The harp plinks of May.
Palms blush in the desert simoom.

Rachel, slender wristwatch at the slender wrist,
Cupping her sex and menacing the brain.
Enemy. But your hand is earth:
Sweet brown, almost timeless, redolent of sex.

Kindly earring approaches. In Charme d'Orsay.
The daffodils are so beautiful.
A yellow gape, with meadows at their feet.

O blond! O summer of that nape. O
Jessamine-drenched pulse-points.
I am fond of you. I stroke
Your shoulder. Let's go:

Tyrrhenian Sea. A conspirative blue.
Doric temples. The plains
Pregnant with roses. Fields
Die asphodel deaths.

Lips abuzz and deeply filled as goblets,
As though the blood first hesitated at the sweet spot,
Then coursed through the first autumn of a mouth.

O weary head. Invalid, deep in the mourning
Of your swart brows. Smile, brighten, why don't you:
The violins are sawing a rainbow.

Spa Concert

Quite transcending the cripples and the spa proles,
The parasols, lapdogs and feather boas,
The autumn sea and the wretched Grieg,
The question: Will Iris come?

She is cold. The little cane in her hand
Is cold. Shivers. Wants to shrink into her hand.

You, with bluebells woven in your scarf,
The white cross of your parted hair and teeth
Contrasts so prettily with your tan when you laugh!

You white, cliffy land! Marmoreal light!
You make my blood drunk! Bright bay!

The great lassitude of the shoulder-blades!
The tenderness of the skirts about her knees!
O pink dust! Dragonfly coast!
You, ascending steeply off the planes of a hollow.
In violet loincloth. Rowdily breast-crested.

O autumn and homecoming over the sea!
The gardens subside. Grey strand without power.
No boat, no sail abroad.
Who will take me in for the winter?
Blown together from so many distances,
Reconfigured on so many stars
Before this shore. Iris goes.

Caryatid

Renege on the rock! Smash
The oppressor cave! Sashay
Out on to the floor! Scorn the cornices –
See, from the beard of drunk Silenus,
From the unique uproar of his blood,
The wine dribble into his genitals!

Spit on the obsession with pillars:
Ancient rheumatic hands quake toward
Grey skies. Bring down the temple
By the yearning of your knees
Twitching with dance.

Spill, spread, unpetal, bleed
Your soft flowers through great wounds.
Venus with her doves
Girds her loins with roses –
See the summer's last puff of blue
Drift on seas of asters to distant
Tree-brown coasts; see
This final hour of our mendacious
Southern happiness
Held aloft.

1922–1936

Jena

'Jena before us in the lovely valley'
Thus my mother on a postcard
From a walking holiday on the banks of the Saale,
She was spending a week at the spa of Kosen;
Long forgotten now, the ancestor no more,
Her script a subject for graphology,
Years of becoming, years of illusion,
Only those words I'll never forget.

It wasn't a great picture, no class,
There was not enough blossom
To justify lovely, poor paper, no pulp-free mass,
Also the hills weren't green with vineyards,
But she was from back-country hovels,
So the valleys probably did strike her as lovely,
She didn't need laid paper or four-colour print,
She supposed others would see what she had seen.

It was something said at a venture,
An exaltation had prompted it,
The landscape had moved her,
So she asked the waiter for a postcard,
And yet – *vide supra* – the ancestor went on,
As will we all, including even those –
Years of becoming, years of illusion –
Who see the town in the valley today.

Never Lonelier

Never lonelier than in August:
Hour of plenitude – the countryside
Waving with red and golden tassels,
But where is your pleasure garden?

Soft skies and sparkling lakes,
The healthy sheen of fields,
But where is the pomp and display
Of the empire you represent?

Everything lays claim to happiness,
Swaps glances, swaps rings
In wine-breath, in the intoxication of things;
You serve the counter-happiness, the intellect.

Asters

Asters – sweltering days
Old adjuration / curse,
The gods hold the balance
For an uncertain hour.

Once more the golden flocks
Of heaven, the light, the trim –
What is the ancient process
Hatching under its dying wings?

Once more the yearned-for,
The intoxication, the rose of you,
Summer leaned in the doorway
Watching the swallows,

One more presentiment
Where certainty is not hard to come by:
Wing tips brush the face of the waters,
Swallows sip speed and night.

Turin

'I'm on my uppers,'
Wrote world-class genius
In his last letter – then they haul
Him off to Jena – psychiatry calls.

I can't afford to buy books;
I sit around in public libraries,
Scribble notes, then go for a sandwich,
These are the days of Turin.

While Europe's noble rot
Supped at Pau, Bayreuth and Epsom,
He put his arms round two cart-
horses, until his landlord dragged him home.

1937–1947

Ah, the faraway land –

Ah, the faraway land,
where heartbreak
comes to rest
dragonfly-fleetingly
on round pebble
or murmurous reed-bed,
and the moon
with its oblique light
– half frost, half cream of wheat –
casts the background of night
into such soothing relief –

ah, the faraway land,
where the hills are warmed
by the shimmering reflection of the lakes,
as for instance Asolo, where la Duse slumbers –
when the *Duilio* carried her home from Pittsburgh,
all the warships, even the British, flagged at
    half-mast
as she passed through the Straits –

self-communing there
without taking in anything to hand,
sense of selfhood,
early mechanisms,
totem fragments
in the soft air –

an end of raisin-bread in your coat –
and so the days pass,
till there stands out against the sky the bough
on which the birds rest,
their long flight done.

Chopin

Not much of a conversationalist,
ideas weren't his strong suit,
ideas miss the point,
when Delacroix expounded his theories
it made him nervous, he for his part
could offer no explanation of the Nocturnes.

A poor lover;
mere shadow in Nohant
where George Sand's children
rejected his attempts
at discipline.

His tuberculosis
took the chronic form,
with repeated bleeding and scarring;
a creeping death,
as opposed to one
in convulsions of agony
or by firing squad:
the piano (Erard) was pushed back against the door
and Delphine Potocka
sang him
Mozart's *Veilchenlied* in his last hour.

He took three pianos with him to England:
Pleyel, Erard, Broadwood,
for twenty guineas
he would give fifteen-minute recitals in the evenings
at the Rothschilds' and the Wellingtons', in Strafford
    House
to the assembled cummerbunds;
then, dark with fatigue and imminent death,
he went home
to the Square d'Orleans.

There he burned his sketches
and manuscripts,
didn't want any leftover scraps
betraying him –
at the end he said:
'I have taken my experiment
as far as it was possible for me to go.'

Each finger was to play
to no more than its natural strength,
the fourth being the weakest
(twinned with the middle finger).
At the start, they occupied the keys
of E, F sharp, G sharp, B and C.

Anyone hearing
certain of his Preludes
in country seats or
at altitude,
through open French windows
on the terrace, say, of a sanatorium,
will not easily forget it.

He composed no operas,
no symphonies,
only those tragic progressions
from artistic conviction
and with a small hand.

Death of Orpheus

How can you leave me, darling –
sent packing by the nether slopes of Erebus
to drift around the inhospitable forests
of Rhodope,
parti-coloured berries,
red-glowing fruit –
gathering foliage,
striking the lyre,
my thumb on the strings!

Three years in the biting north wind!
To think of the dead is sweet,
my so-removed one,
I hear your voice more clearly,
feel your kisses,
both the fleeting and the thorough –
but the thought of you among the shades!

How can you leave me
to the naiads' onslaught,
the blandishments of the cliff-face beauties,
their cooing: 'in the bleak woods
only fauns and wood-sprites, but you,
singer of bronze light,
constellator of swallow-teeming skies –
put away your song –
forget!'

– threaten – !

One sends me such meaning looks.
And another, well-built, freckled,
probably mixed-race ('it's called yellow poppy'),
beckons demurely, suggests chaste games
and means rampant desire – ('inspect my love
    chalice's
purple!' – forget it, baby!)

– they threaten – !

No, you're not to be diluted,
you're not to blur
into Iole, Dryope, Procne,
nor mix your features with Atalanta's,
I don't want to blurt out your name inappropriately
when I'm with some Laïs –

but: they threaten me – !

and now the stones
no more obedient to my voice,
the singer's,
no more swaddling themselves in moss,
cudgels not soothed with leafage,
no scythes muffled with ears of corn –
naked flails – !

helpless now against the whelps of bitches,
the merciless –
lashes wet,
gums bloodied –

and now the lyre –
downstream –

the echoing banks –

September

I

You, leaning over the fence and the phlox
(split by the rain,
smelling strangely feral),
given to walking on stubble fields,
going up to old people
plucking balsamines,
inhaling smoke on ploughland
with pleasure and sorrow –

walls going up
meaning to be roofed before the onset of snow and winter,
apprentices slaking lime,
calling out to them: 'Why bother,'
then shyly stifling it –

squat, not lofty,
and a shapeless pumpkin by your foot,
fat and featureless, blebbed growth –

escapee from the plains,
terminal moon of flame,
shrivelling from fruit- and fever-swellings,
already dark-complexioned –
fool or baptist,
summer's fool, babbler, obit
or hymn to glaciers,
in any case nut-cracker,
reed-mower,
purveyor of self-evident truths –

before you the snow,
profound silence,
unfruitful expanses.
You reach out for it,
but leaning over the fence,
seethe of weed and beetle,
the lust for life
of spiders and field-mice.

II

You, mountain-ash hung
from Indian summer,
stubbly ghost,
cabbage whites in your breath,
let many hands tick,
cuckoo clocks strike,
bells din for evensong,
gong
the hour so fixed and golden,
so definitively weathered,
into a trembling heart!

You – other!
Only gods
or tunics

of invincible Titans
rest so,
long-made,
so deeply sewn into
the tracks of flowers and moths!

Or slumber of an earlier kind,
when there was no awakening,
only golden warmth and purple berries
nibbled by perennial swallows
that never migrate –
Sound it, gong it,
this hour,
because when you cease,
the edges of the fields will encroach,
poplar-grown and chill.

Tracing

O those years! The green light of morning
and the still unswept pavements –
summer yelled from every surface of the city
and supped at a horn
refilled from above.

Silent hour. Watery colours
of a pale green eye's diluted stream,
scenes picked out in that magic green, glass dances,
shepherds and ponds, pigeons, a cupola –
woven, dispatched, shining, faded –
mutable clouds of happiness!

So you faced the day: the font
without bubbles, the frontages
loom without you; the houses
locked, it was for you to create
the morning, early jasmine,
its yelps, its incipient aboriginal
stream – still without end – O the years!

Something unquenchable in the heart,
playing to you from reeds and gardens,
complement to heaven and earth;
evening storms
drenched the brassy umbels,
darkly they burst, taut with seeds,
and sea and strands,
wimpled with tents,

full of burning sand,
weeks bronzing, tanning everything
to leather for kisses landing
indiscriminately like cloudbursts
and soon over!

Above hung a weight
even then – but grapes
from it,

pulling down the tendrils and letting them rebound,
only a few berries
if you wanted,
first –

not yet so bulging and overhung with
plate-sized bunches,
old heavy grape-flesh –

O the years!

II

Dark days of spring,
unyielding murk in the leaves;
drooping lilac barely looking up,
narcissus colour, and smelling strongly of death,
loss of content,
untriumphant sadness of the unfulfilled.

And in the rain
falling on the leaves,
I hear an old song –
of forests once crossed
and revisited, but not
the hall where they were singing,
the keys were silent,
the hands were resting somewhere
apart from the arms that held me,
moved me to tears,
hands from the eastern steppes,
long since trampled and bloody –
only their singing
in the rain
dark days of spring
everlasting steppes.

St Petersburg – Mid-Century

'Each of you who helps another
is Gethsemane,
each of you who comforts another
is the mouth of Christ,'
they sing in St Isaac's Cathedral,
the Alexander Nevsky Monastery,
the church of Peter and Paul
where the emperors rest,
and in the remaining one hundred and twenty-nine
    Orthodox,
eight Roman Catholic,
one Anglican, three Armenian,
Lithuanian, Swedish, Estonian
and Finnish chapels.

Blessing
of the clear blue Neva
on the day of Three Kings.
The water is very healthy, it washes away all impurities.
Ferries the wonderful treasures
for the Mother-of-Pearl Room,
the Amber Room
in Tsarskoye Selo
in the Duderhoff Hills,
the sky-blue Siberian marble
for the steps.
Twenty-one gun salutes
when the ice melts,
the daughter of Lakes
Onega and Ladoga!

Morning concert in the Engelhardt Room,
Mme Stepanov,
who has created Glinka's 'Life for the Tsar'
screams unnaturally,
Voroyev's baritone has suffered.
Leaning against a pillar,
with protuberant white teeth,
thick African lips,
browless,
stands Alexander Sergeyevich (Pushkin).

Beside him Baron Brambeus
whose 'great reception at Satan's'
is accounted the height of perfection.
Cellist: Davidoff.
And then the Russian basses: extra low,
often a full octave below the standard basses,
the counter-C pure and clear
from twenty throats,
extra low.

To the islands!
Krestovsky – cesspool of vice! –
Bashkirs, bearded Russians, reindeer Samoyed
for purposes of sensuality and hyper-sensuality!
First part:
'From the gorilla to the destruction of God,'
second part:
'From the destruction of God to the transformation
of physical man'.

Also grain vodka!
The end of things –
vodka hiccups
extra low!

Raskolnikov
(ontologically under strain)
sets foot in Kabak,
a low bar.
Sticky tables,
harmonica,
all-day drinkers,
bags under their eyes,
one of them invites him
'to a sensible conversation,'
hayseeds in his hair.
(Another murderer:
Dorian Grey, Esq., London,
smell of lilac,
honey-coloured laburnum
beside the house – a Park Lane dream –
examines a Ceylon ruby for Lady B.,
orders up a gamelan orchestra.)

Raskolnikov,
stiff,
is wakened by Sonia 'with the yellow ticket'
(a prostitute. Her father
is 'surprisingly relaxed' about her calling),
she says:

'Get up! Come with me now!
Stand at the crossroads,
kiss the ground you soiled,
where you sinned,
then bow before all the world,
tell everyone aloud:
I am the murderer –
will you do that?
Will you come? –
And he came.

Anyone who comforts another
is the mouth of Christ.

Static Poems

Aversion to progress
is profundity in the wise man,
children and grandchildren
don't bother him,
don't alarm him.

To represent a particular outlook,
to act,
to travel hither and yon
are all signs of a world
that doesn't see clearly.
In front of my window
– wise man says –
is a valley
where shadows pool,
two poplars mark a path,
leading you will know where to.

Perspective
is another word for stasis:
you draw lines,
they ramify
like a creeper –
tendrils explode –
and they disburse crows in swarms
in the winter red of early dawns

then let them settle –

you will know – for whom.

1949–1955

Evenings of Certain Lives

I

You don't need to be always scrubbing the tiles,
   Hendrickje,
my eye drinks itself,
drinks itself to death –
but other drink is in short supply –
the little Buddha there,
Chinese grove god
in exchange for a ladleful of Hulstkamp,
please!

Never painted anything
in frost-white or ice-skater blue
or that Irish green
with the purple shimmering through –
always my own monotone,
my compulsion to shadows –
not pleasant
to pursue that path so clearly.

Greatness – how so?
I pick up the slate-pencil and certain things appear
on paper or canvas
or whatever the heck else –
result: bronze Buddha hocked for booze –
but I draw the line at homages under ornamental
   plants,
banquet of the painters' guild –
something for the boardroom!

[49]

. . . Creaking,
little sheep squeaks, chromotypes
Flemish, Rubensish –
for the grandchildren
(same idiots!)

Ah – Hulstkamp,
hits the spot,
mid-point of colours,
my shadow brown,
stubble aura around heart and eye.

II

The blocked chimney smokes
– the Swan of Avon blows his nose –
the tree stumps are sodden,
clammy night, emptiness mingled with draft –
enough characters,
the world is overpopulated as it is,
plentiful peach-fall, four rosebuds
per annum –
asperged,
set to tread the boards
by this hand,
grown wrinkled
and with sluggish veins!

All those Juliets and Ophelias,
wreathed, silvered, sometimes murderous –
all the soft mouths, the sighs
I extracted from them –
the original actresses long since turned to smoke,
rust, leeched dry, rats' pudding –
heart's Ariel too, away with the elements.

The age takes off its frockcoat.
These lousy skulls of lords,
their trains of thought
that I pushed into extremes –
my lords makers of history
all of them crowned and sceptred illiterates,
great powers of the cosmos –
yes, like so many bats or kites!

Sir Goon wrote to me lately:
'the rest is silence' –
I think that's one of mine,
could only be mine,
Dante dead – lacuna
of centuries
to my concordance –

what if they didn't exist,
the booty never brought to light,
the booths, the scaffolds, the cymbals
never clashed –
gaps? Gap teeth maybe,
but the great monkey jaws
would grind on
emptiness, mingled with draft –
the tree stumps are sodden
and the butler snores in porter dreams.

A Shadow on the Wall

A shadow on the wall
boughs stirred by the noonday wind
that's enough earth
and for the eye
enough celestial participation.

How much further do you want to go? Refuse
the bossy insistence
of new impressions –

lie there still,
behold your own fields,
your estate,
dwelling especially
on the poppies,
unforgettable
because they transported the summer –

where did it go?

Fragments

Fragments,
soul flotsam,
coagulates of the twentieth century –

scars – break in flow from the dawn of creation,
the historical religions of five centuries in smithereens,
science: cracks in the Parthenon,
Planck blending with Kepler and Kierkegaard,
the fresh murk of his quantum theory –

but there were evenings robed in the colours
of the Almighty, loose, flowing,
incontrovertible in the silence
of their streaming blues,
colour of introverts,
there I sat
hands spread on my knees
like a farmer,
quietly nursing my drink
while the labourers played harmonicas –

and others
are driven by inner whorls,
convolutes,
architectonic compressions
or amours.

Crises of expression and spasms of eros:
that's the man of today,
the inside a vacuum,
the continuity of personality
held together by his suit,
which with stout cloth might be good for ten years.

The rest fragments,
mi-voix,
snatches of melody from next door,
Negro spirituals
or Ave Marias.

Think of the Unsatisfied Ones

When despair –
you who enjoyed great triumphs
and walked with confidence and the memory
of many gifts of delirium and dawns
and unexpected
turns –
when despair wants you in its grip,
and threatens you from some unfathomable depth
with destruction
and the guttering out of your flame:

then think of the unsatisfied ones,
with their migraine-prone temples and introverted
    dispositions,
loyal to a few memories
that held out little hope,
who still bought flowers
and with a smile of not much candle power
confided secret desires
to their small-scale heavens –
soon extinguished.

Syntax

We all have the sky, and love, and the grave,
that's not at issue,
that's been chewed over and done to death in illustrated
    lecture-series.
But what's new is the question of syntax
and that's urgent:
what makes us try to give expression to anything?

Why rhyme, or sketch a girl
either face to face or her mirror image,
or brush thicknesses of expensive laid paper
with innumerable plants, treetops, walls,
these last in the form of fat caterpillars with tortoise heads
creeping low to the ground
in fixed dispositions?

Overwhelmingly unanswerable!
Not the prospect of payment,
many starve in the process. No,
it's an impulse of the remote-controlled
hand, a condition of the brain,
perhaps a delayed Messiah or shamanic animal,
a priapism of form at the expense of content,
it will pass,
but today syntax
is primary.

'The few who understood anything about it?' – (Goethe) –
about what?
I imagine: about syntax.

Finis Poloniae

Finis Poloniae –
a phrase / figure of speech,
that apart from its literal historical meaning
stands in for
the end of empires.

Charged atmosphere,
everything breathes damply,
epicene air – if it could think anything
it would think un-European things like monsoons
and yellow seas.

Greatness bears itself to death,
says its last words to itself,
a foreign-sounding swansong, generally misunderstood,
sometimes tolerated –

Finis Poloniae –
perhaps on a rainy day, bummer,
but in this instance a sound of happiness
followed by solo horn,
and then a hydrangea, most placid of flowers,
capable of standing out in the rain into November,
dropped softly into the grave.

Nocturne

From the saloon bar the rattle of dice on a wooden
    table top,
beside you a couple at the anthropophagous stage,
a chestnut bough on the piano
adds a natural touch,
all in all, my kind of place.

There thought processes settle,
the nausea that exercised
your medulla oblongata all day
is allayed in a fog of alcohol –
at last soul fades and existence dims!

Treading water –
of course you might go down,
but that's a time question –
and time – before oceans?
They were there first,
before consciousness and conception,
no one went angling for monsters,
no one suffered deeper than ten feet,
which if you think about it isn't so very much.

Gladioli

A bunch of glads,
certainly highly emblematic of creation,
remote from frills of working blossom with hope of
    fruit –
slow, durable, placid,
generous, sure of kingly dreams.

All else is natural world and intellect!
Over there the mutton herds:
strenuous ends of clover and daggy sheep –
here friendly talents,
pushing Anna to the centre of attention,
explaining her, finding a solution!

The glads offer no solution:
being – falling –
you mustn't count the days –
fulfilment
livid, tattered, or beautiful.

Restaurant

The gentleman over there orders another pint,
well, that's nice, then I don't need to worry
if I have another myself in due course.
Trouble is, one straightaway thinks one is addicted,
I even read in an American magazine
that every cigarette you smoke takes thirty-six minutes
    off your life,
I don't believe that, presumably it's the chewing gum
    industry
that's behind that, or Coca-Cola.

A normal life and a normal death –
I don't know what they're good for. Even a normal life
ends in an unhealthy death. Altogether death
doesn't have a lot to do with health and sickness,
it merely uses them for its own purposes.

What do you mean: death doesn't have a lot to do with
    sickness?
I mean this: a lot of people get sick without dying,
so what we have before us is something different,
the introduction of a variable,
a source of uncertainty,
not an open and shut case,
not the grim reaper mounted on a bag of bones,
but something that observes, sees round corners,
    exercises restraint,
and musically plays a different tune.

Blue Hour

I

I enter the deep blue hour –
here is the landing, the chain shuts behind
and now in the room only carmine on a mouth
and a bowl of late roses – you!

We both know, those words
that we both spoke and often offered others
are of no account and out of place between us:
this is everything and endgame.

Silence has advanced so far
it fills the room and seals it shut
the hour – nothing hoped and nothing suffered –
with its bowl of late roses – you.

II

Your face blurs, is white and fragile,
meanwhile there collects on your mouth
all of desire, the purple and the blossoms
from some ancestral flotsam stock.

You are so pale, I think you might founder
in a snowdrift, in unblooming
deathly-white roses, one by one – coral
only on your lips, heavy and like a wound.

You are so soft, you portend something
of happiness, of submersion and danger
in a blue, a deep blue hour
and when it's gone, no one knows if it was.

III

I remind you, you are another's,
what are you doing bearing me these late roses?
You say dreams bleach, hours wander,
what is all this: he and I and you?

'What arises and arouses, it all comes to an end,
what happens – who exactly knows,
the chain falls shut, we are silent in these walls,
and outside is all of space, lofty and dark blue.'

Theoretical Afterlife?

Soon through,
out of time,
a man prematurely or otherwise deceased,
of whom people speak the way they speak of a singer
with a clapped out soprano
or little Hölty with his few ditties –
less than that: just par,
never went up in a plane,
never took the wheel of a Borgward –
a dime for the streetcar,
at most, transfer.

But so much went by you every day,
introverted, extroverted,
existential worries, marital strife, tax issues –
with all of that you had to concern yourself,
a pile of life in variegated forms.

On a postcard from Antibes
that arrived today
a castle soars into the Med,
a freakish object:
the south, the sea, snow-capped mountains on the
    periphery –
a dramatization of centuries
soars, rests, shines, glamours, obtrudes
into the snap –

none of all that *chez toi,*
not so much as the wherewithal for a postcard –
a dime for the streetcar,
transfer,
and soon enough the words above:
out of time.

Still Life

When everything lies there in fallen heaps
thoughts, moods, duets
– lies there despoiled
without tin foil – and the scraped membrane
– all the layers washed away –
of the bloody conjunctiva stares into silence –
what's left?

The sixty-four thousand dollar question! But who in
     his senses
asks it any more –
Renaissance reminiscences,
Baroque overlay,
castle museums –

an end to drilling,
but still no ground water,
the wells dark,
the styles exhausted –

time has acquired a stillness,
the hour breathes
over a wine jug,
it's late, the last blows have been traded,
a clinch and a hang on the ropes
before the bell – I give the world
to anyone who wants it, let them be happy:

the jester's not to turn serious
the drinker's not to wander into the Gobi desert
even a lady with lorgnette
entertains aspirations to happiness:
well, let her –

the lake rests at ease
rimmed with forget-me-nots,
adders laugh.

Encounters

Such encounters these days
ripe, golden, peach-curved,
where the sun's brides (Helenium)
still carry effective colours into the garden –
heavy with age /
light with age,
where even the teardrop says: 'Chin up!
It's not so bad, and not long to go!'

Encounters, for instance dusk,
l'heure bleue, creation trembles with samba,
the gentleman lays his hand
between his partner's shoulder-blades,
all over the world from Fiesole to La Paz
sensuality and joy –

or the songs of the Ohio River,
hanging in the trees,
in reeds and dreams
of youth, on the cusp of life –
how soon, and how long – ?

Yellow of strand and blue of night
and on the coral reef the white yacht,
whatever was in you of dream and myth,
you behold from your hotel window in Denpasar –

encounters lacking a centre,
no father and no child,
encounters of a peachy complexion
with a sun's bride in heaven's corridor,
encounters – the early and the late,
the torch of existence passed from hand to hand.

Hymn

That quality of the great boxers
to be able to stand there
and take shots,

gargle with firewater,
encounter intoxication
at sub- and supra-atomic levels,
to leave one's sandals at the crater's lip
like Empedocles, and descend,

not say: I'll be back,
not think: fifty-fifty,
to vacate molehills
when dwarves want space to grow,
to dine alone,
indivisible,
and able to renounce your victory –

a hymn to that man.

What's Bad

Not reading English,
and hearing about a new English thriller
that hasn't been translated.

Seeing a cold beer when it's hot out,
and not being to afford it.

Having an idea
that you can't encapsulate in a line of Hölderlin,
the way the professors do.

Hearing the waves beat against the shore on holiday
    at night,
and telling yourself it's what they always do.

Very bad: being invited out,
when your own room at home is quieter,
the coffee is better,
and you don't have to make small talk.

And worst of all:
not to die in summer,
when the days are long
and the earth yields easily to the spade.

Foreign Ministers

Considered as a whole,
the nations are worth a Mass,
but individually: let trumpet speak to drum,
the King drinks to Hamlet –
a terrific scene,
but the foils are poisoned.

'Izwolski laughed.'
Quotes at his fingertips, bonmots up his sleeve,
now frosty, now charming, peace and goodwill,
better one toot on the flute too many,
Count Witte's glad-handing in Portsmouth (1905)
broke all records, but the terms were more favourable.

To parliament – by no means bunkum,
there's a method to it just as there is in Sanskrit or particle
    physics,
and a huge staff besides: researchers, press office, spear-
    carriers,
and you have to be able to feel the man's character
through the whole: seriously high flyers have it,
not through some processes or other,
but the moral equivalent of sex appeal –
and then: what is a state anyway?
The actuality of the ethical idea,
according to Plato.

'Dichotomy between public
and private opinion' (Keynes). Opalesce!
You live in the divide between the high-ups and the others,
first COO, then obscure posting in the Balkans,
finally boss,
then a reshuffle,
and you retire to your estate.
Easily said: mistaken political direction.
Mistaken when? Today? In ten years? Next century?

Mésalliances, treachery, intrigues,
all at our expense,
be sure you slip on a sou'wester
before you go out,
check whether the eagles are flying left or right,
if the sacred pullets are off their feed.
When Hannibal came over the Simplon with his elephants,
everything looked plain sailing,
later, when Carthage fell,
Salammbo wept.

Socialism – Capitalism – if the grape grows,
and the national economy converts its juice
by means of certain extraordinary inventions and
    manipulations
to *mousseux* – then someone has to drink it, no?
Or should we blame the Celts
for carrying off the Massilian stock
back to Gaul with them by way of exchange –
that would be to condemn history, progress,
and the spread of cultures.

'At the end of a two-hour meeting,
the foreign ministers came to a provisional agreement'
(oil and pipeline questions),
three wore tails,
one was in a burnoose.

Dream

I had just read 'Bus-stop
and Biography' in the newspaper
when two figures emerged from the forest
both long-dead,
kitted out with top hats and rucksacks

not at the same time
but on two successive days
old acquaintances, yes, family-members
I asked them where they were going at this unwonted
hour of life or, rather, death,
but they only looked up crossly
and one of them remarked
he was going to spend several weeks with an
apothecary.

A reserved pair,
their features indicated
cross-connections
surprises
changes of plan

I knew as little as before,
as before bus-stop and biography.

Despair

Things you said in drugstores
when buying painkillers
or at your tailor's
apart from details of measurements or cut –
brouillons of chitchat,
in what way did they ever express you?

In the morning – still shattered
from the palaver of getting up –
things babbled, so as not to stagger off in silence,
this and that, bits of news,
general truths, all mixed up –
the general truths were always your forte!
Where is the seat of that in you? In your gut? Since when?
And what is it anyway? Source of instinct, cement of optimism,
                              economic speculation –
certainly something incredibly flimsy!

All of it totted up
from morning and night-time hours,
in civvies and in uniform
makes you vomit with its superfluousness
as you look back, dead words, hollow sounds,
no connection with anything –

or is it here that human fellowship begins?

All the ruses,
the shameless grinning in the face of someone
you want on your side,
but without telling them the truth about you,
without revealing the coarseness, the ogling, the betrayal,
mainly because you don't really know
what ogling and betrayal are,
that whole tissue of cunning, unmannerliness and semi-tears.

Kürten in Dusseldorf –
from 7 till 9 engaged in rape and murder,
but all the rest of the time bowling club member and
    paterfamilias –
wasn't that reasonable
and in keeping with *Pithecanthropus erectus?*

Culture clubs may come and go,
orient, occident and accident,
cave drawings, feisty Madonnas,
hermaphroditic equipment,
plein-air sodomy –
all comes and goes and no one thinks it through
to the gods,
to the finish.

So smile, use scented soap
when you run to your mistress,
and grease your skin before you shave;
that keeps it supple.

III

When you talk to yourself, you talk to the things
and of the things, that are so bitter,
no other conversation is possible,
both bear death, both end blind.

Here the east sings and the west sinks pints,
fruit explodes with ripeness,
ooze from palm and gum tree
even the orchid runs with individual juice.

You all over, you once again open to all,
the final hour, and you soar and soar,
then one more song, and beautifully hit,
you sink, you know existence, and you hold your peace.

'Broadway Sings and Dances'
a magnifique reportage!

1. The debut of the black singer
(hitherto known for her work in lieder and aria)
as the fortune teller Ulrica in *The Masked Ball*,
now with full-scale orchestral backing and famous voices:
'a resounding triumph.'

2. Incidents, dramatised: trimmers the lot of them,
just one instance of 'trying
to bring truth to light'
'in the teeth of majority opinion'
(splendid – but see also Pontius Pilate).

3. Dowager Empress and the Princess Irina:
a contest fraught with almost unbearable inner (!)
tension,
then three conmen show up
(an unbeatable formula!).

4. Noah and his brood – the whole story of the Flood
the voyage of the Ark till landfall,
the 'celebrated patriarch'
his attitude 'in every sense profound',
'literally stunning,'
the songs were played to the lyricist
by phone from New York to St Moritz
(golly gosh! Noah's Ark songs!).

As against our Europe! Ur-stamping ground of the spirit as
    may be,
but so much pretentious twaddle:
'The Truth,' a life's work, 500 pages –
the truth can't be that long!
Or:
'Philosophy for Philosophers',
whatever it is it won't be so 'literally stunning'
as Noah on Broadway.

Remember: sketch!

Boy, oh boy!

Impromptu

On the radio someone was singing
'Die Drosselgass' zu Rüdesheim' –
I was stunned:
thrushes, that seems to imply a spring day,
who knows what dangling over the walls,
unbundling, twittering, something in light green for sure –
my heart leapt, not the old one of today
but the young one, tired and exhilarated
at the end of a day's hike.

Even if you didn't drink wine,
you poured yourself something golden in a glass,
brushed the dust from your coat,
and flopped down on a pallet,
with your rucksack jammed under your head,
neither of them with anything in them
except what you needed
for the morrow.

A pair of shoes. A son of the Muses.
Back then, Liliencron was my God,
and I wrote him a postcard.

Bauxite

I spent a lot of money this week,
almost four hundred marks,
but it did make possible some magical moments,
sublime, interior, silksoft,
with flows of intoxicating transcendence.

I often study
an individual's right hand:
it's the hand that opens,
usually it's not worth the candle,
but the times that you remember
are the blisses of the deeply breathing
soft white chestnut flowers
that are a blessing in May.

From other tables one hears: 'We're tutti players,'
or 'Herr Kraft, what good are customers
who don't pay their promissory notes,'
or 'The monthly instalments are thirteen-fifty':
the world is full of such speech.
And confronting them the encashments of heaven,
ruinous perhaps, in a certain sense criminal,
but you were lying around shop-soiled, grubby, sale item,
and now for four hundred marks
cracks in the rocks
detonations

the veins shimmer
with pure gold
bauxite –

an entire week for heaven's 'tutti players.'

Only fleeting now

Only fleeting now,
no Orplid, nowhere permanent,
figures / disfigurements
abrupt,
curtailed.

Serge Rubinstein
sank
two million dollars
in skinny, voluptuous, strict,
blue- and murky-eyed
ladies, chorus girls, dentists' receptionists and vamps,
the sticking plaster on his conk
when he was strangled
was scanned for fingerprints,
but provided no leads.

Only fleeting now –
it's the turn of the Andes:
aboriginal, wrinkled,
nothing for geodesists,
no *nous*
no Muses
edge world
look further –
yields beets!
yields potato fields!

yields litres of God,
yards of Hell,
yields grooves
to record
to arrest
to nest in, one would fain cry –
nothing –
yields grooves!

Only fleeting now
neuralgia in the morning
hallucinations at night
propped on alcohol and cigarettes

occluded genes
frozen chromosomes,
the crutch perspires a little
to the boogie-woogie,
then the trousers are returned to their press.

Where is anything resolved,
where does anything shine from afar,
no Orplid –
culture club:
Pye plus rope tricks!

Left the House

I

Left the house shattered, it hurt so bad,
so many years as a man, compromise,
in spite of partial success in intellectual tussle
he was never anyone of Olympian allure.

He walked slowly through the dreamscape
of the late autumn day, barely distinguishable
from early spring, with young willows
and a patch of waste ground where blue jays
   screamed.

Dreamy exposure to phenomena
that to nature in its administration
of various cycles – young and old alike –
are inseparably part of a single order –

so he drank his gin and accepted a dish
of sausage soup (free on Thursdays
with a beverage), and so found the Olympian balance
of sorrow and pleasure.

II

He had been reading on the park bench
and stared into the last roses' grey,
there were no titans, just shrubs
thinned out by fall.

He set aside his book. It was a day like any other
and the people were like all people everywhere,
that was how it would always be, at least
this mixture of death and laughter would persist.

A scent is enough to change things,
even small flowers stand in some relation to a cedar of
    Lebanon,
then he walked on and saw the windows of the
    furriers
were full of warm things for the winter ahead.

III

All very well, a gin and a few minutes
in the park at noon, with the sun shining,
but what about when the landlord comes by, and there
    are problems
with your tax return, and the girlfriend's in tears?

Shattered: how far are you allowed to push your I,
and see personal things as somehow symptomatic?
Shattered: to what extent are you obliged to play by
    the rules –
as far as a Ludwig Richter canvas?

Shattered: no one knows. Shattered and you turn
equally pained to singular and universal –
your little experiment with destiny will end
gloriously and forever, but quite alone.

Damned evergreens! Vinyl whines!
Gin, sun, cedars – what use are they
to help the self reconcile landlord, God, and dream –
voices warble and words mock –
left the house and closed his reverie.

People Met

I have met people who,
asked after their names,
shyly – as if they had no title
to an appellation all to themselves –
replied 'Fräulein Christian' and added:
'like the first name,' they wanted make it easy for the
     other,
not a difficult name like 'Popiol' or 'Babendererde' –
'like the first name' – please, don't burden your memory
     overmuch!

I have met people who
grew up in a single room with their parents
and four brothers and sisters, and studied at night
with their fingers in their ears at the kitchen table,
and still grew up to be beautiful and self-possessed as
     duchesses –
and innerly gentle and hard-working as Nausicaa,
clear-browed as angels.

I have often asked myself and never found an answer
whence kindness and gentleness come,
I don't know it to this day, and now must go myself.

Rowans

Rowans – not yet fully rowan red
not yet in that tone they take on later
of ember, berry, October and death.

Rowans – still a little green about the gills,
but see them bundled into a leggy bouquet,
making their *sotto voce* farewells:
maybe never again, chum, or just this once.

Rowans – this year and all the years,
first that queasy greenish-pink and then rowan red,
coloured up, plumped, ripened, and offered to God –
but where was it you plumped, coloured, and ripened?

Last Spring

Fill yourself up with the forsythias
and when the lilacs flower, stir them in too
with your blood and happiness and wretchedness,
the dark ground that seems to come with you.

Sluggish days. All obstacles overcome.
And if you say, ending or beginning, who knows,
then maybe – just maybe – the hours will carry you
into June, when roses blow.

Late

The big old trees
in the parks,
and the flower beds
all damp and tangled –

autumnal sweetness,
tuffets of erica
along the Autobahn,
everything is Lüneburg
heather, purple and unbearing,
whins going nowhere,
introverted stuff
soon browned off –
give it a month
it'll be as if it'd never flowered.

So much for nature.
And through the city
in the blinking light
beer trucks deliver ataraxy,
unconcern with thirst and desires –
what is it doesn't quench itself?
Only small circles!
The big ones wallow
in excess.

II

Memory comes down to this:
fields and lakes fused with your days,
early tunes
on an old piano.

Shy souls! Youth!
Then, seemingly all by themselves,
infidelity, lapse, slip from grace –
the backgrounds to bliss.

And love.
'I do believe you really wanted to stay with me,
but weren't able to.
I don't blame you for what happened,'
yes, love,
heavy and variegated,
after keeping our secret for years
we will call out to one another: 'Don't forget,'
till one of us is dead –
so the roses go,
petal by petal.

III

To be as one once was:
irresponsible, no knowledge of how things end,
be guided by the flesh: thirst, tenderness, conquest, loss,
the reaching across into the other – whomever or whatever.

To sit there of an evening, staring down night's throat,
a narrowing funnel, but at the bottom are flowers,
scent climbs, trembly and brief,
followed of course by putrefaction,
then it's completely dark, and you remember what you came for,
and put down your money and leave –

loved so many lies,
believed so many words
spoken by curved lips
and your own heart
so impulsive, bottomless, changeable –

loved so many lies,
sought so many lips
('oh, wipe the lipstick off your mouth,
give it me pale')

and ever more questions –

IV

Little old lady
in a big red room
little old lady –
hums Marion Davies
while Hearst, her lover of 30 years,
arrives outside the marble orchard
with the protection of a numerous escort
and followed by 22 limousines, lying in a heavy copper coffin
all to the quiet whine of the TV cameras.

Little old lady, big red room,
henna red, plush gladioli red, imperial purple (that wee snail
    in the Med),
the bedroom in the Castle in Santa Monica
done up a la Pompadour –

Louella, she calls, radio!
The blues, jitterbug – zigzag!
Upper classes up and down the Atlantic,
marriageable daughters, obliterated urges,
palazzos on the water, eiderdowns on the mattresses,
the world was divided between rep and demi-rep –
I was always the latter –

Louella, my tincture!
What's it all for –
Humiliation, revival, more, atrocious suffering –
his features, ugly features, now sealed in the copper coffin,

he would crash the lights when he saw me,
even a wealthy man can love and tremble and feel
    hellfire.

Neat – the glass by the silver shaker,
he's silent now, though it's our hour of the day
our private time –
strange things he would say on the phone,
'life gets settled over the breakfast table',
'hailstones feel like granite if you're on the beach in
    swimming-costume',
'the unexpected always happens,
the hoped-for never does – '
those were his moralities.

Constitutional over. Just a few more flagstones,
set the glass down on the last,
neat, plink of ice, last rhapsody,
little old lady,
big red room.

V

Feel it – but remember, millennia have felt it –
the sea and the beasts and the mindless stars
wrestle it down today as ever –

think it – but remember, the most exalted
are wallowing in their own bow-wave,
are no more than the yellow of the buttercup,
while other colours too play their game –

remember and endure the hour,
there was never one like it / all are like it,
people and angels and cherubim,
black-winged, bright-eyed,
none was yours –
was ever yours.

VI

Do you not see how a few stop
and many turn their backs,
strange lean shapes,
all making for the bridges.

Lower their sticks, stop the clock,
the clock face needs no light,
vanishing hordes, black shapes
all weeping, do you not see?

Devastations

Devastations –
but where there's nothing more to devastate,
even the ruins are mellowing,
chicory and plantain sprouting
from tumps of rubble
smooshed to humus –

devastations –
still proclaim: here were once
mass, construction, foundations –
proud word
evocative of
plenitude
and acres of home –

devastations –
grey Rip Van Winkle word
with clouds, showers, gloomy leaf shadow,
and all of long duration –
where summer should have been,
with fruit punch,
dishes of ice cream beaded on the outside,
and beach-parties in the white nights.

They Are Human After All

They are human after all, you think,
as the waiter steps up to a table
out of sight of you,
reserved, corner table –
they too are thin-skinned and pleasure-seeking,
with their own feelings and their own sufferings.

You're not so all alone
in your mess, your restlessness, your shakes,
they too will be full of doubt, dither, shilly-shallying,
even if it's all about making deals,
the universal-human
albeit in its commercial manifestation,
but present there too.

Truly, the grief of hearts is ubiquitous
and unending,
but whether they were ever in love
(outwith the awful wedded bed)
burning, athirst, desert-parched
for the nectar of a faraway
mouth,
sinking, drowning
in the impossibility of a union of souls –

you won't know, nor can you
ask the waiter,
who's just ringing up
another Becks,
always avid for coupons
to quench a thirst of another nature,
though also deep.

Par ci, par là

There were no Gainsboroughs in my parents' house
and no one played Chopin
perfectly philistrous intellectual life
my father had been to the theatre once
in the early century
Wildenbruch's 'Crested Lark'
that was our pabulum
there was nothing else.

All long gone now
grey hearts, grey hair
the garden in Polish hands
the graves *par ci, par là*
but all on the Slavic side
Oder-Neisse Line
inapplicable to the contents of coffins
the children continue to think about them
the spouses too for a while
par ci, par là
till it's time for them to move on
Selah, end of psalm.

Even now in the big city night
café terrace
summer stars
from the next door table
assessments
of hotels in Frankfurt
the ladies frustrated
if their desires had mass
they would each of them weigh twenty stone.

[100]

But the electricity in the air! Balmy night
à la travel brochure and
the girls step out of their pictures
improbable lovelies
legs up to here, a waterfall,
their surrender is something one daren't even begin
to contemplate.

Married couples by comparison disappoint,
don't cut it, fail to clear the net,
he smokes, she twists her rings,
worth considering
the whole relationship between marriage and creativity,
stifling or galvanizing.

Questions, questions! Scribbled nictitations
on a summer night,
there were no Gainsboroughs in my parents' house,
now everything has gone under
the whole thing, *par ci, par là,*
Selah, end of psalm.

No Tears

Roses, Christ knows how they got to be so lovely,
green skies over the city
in the evening
in the ephemerality of the years!

The yearning I have for that time
when one mark thirty was all I had,
yes, I counted them this way and that,
I trimmed my days to fit them,
days, what am I saying days: weeks on bread and plum
    mush
out of earthenware pots
brought from my village,
still under the rush light of native poverty,
how raw everything felt, how tremblingly beautiful!

What good is the lustre conferred by European pundits,
the great name,
the *Pour le Mérite* –
people shoot their cuffs and tool on,

it's only the ephemeral that's beautiful,
looking back, the poverty,
the frowstiness that didn't know what it was,
sobs, and stands in line for its dole,
what a wonderful Hades
that takes away the frowst,
and the pundits both –
please, no tears,
no one say: oh, I was so lonesome.

from UNCOLLECTED AND POSTHUMOUS POEMS

Expressionist!

They won't stamp a medal with your mug shot
the way the Greeks did for Sappho;
if they failed to beat your brains out, that already
is accounted actionable and treason, in Germany

1886

Easter that year at the latest possible date,
the lilac was already in flower along the Elbe,
but to make up for it such a heavy snowfall in the first
   week of December
that the entire rail network
of Northern and Central Germany
was paralysed for weeks.

Paul Heyse publishes a one-act tragedy,
young bride on the eve of her wedding discovers
that the groom once loved her mother,
now long-since dead, but
from her aunt, who raised her,
she still has a phial of morphine:
'do not disturb the gentle agent,'
she sinks back, reaching for his hand,
Theodor (frantic, shouting):
'Lydia! My wife! Take me with you!' –
Title: ''Twixt Cup and Lip.'

The British conquer Mandalay,
open up the wide valley of the Irrawaddy to world trade;
France acquires Madagascar;
the Russians expel Count Alexander
from Bulgaria.

The Association of German Cyclists
has 1500 members.
Güssfeldt becomes the first man to scale
Mont Blanc
via the Grand Mulet.
Borzois from the Perkhino kennels
in the province of Tula,
the ones with the particularly deep blazons on their
    chest,
used in the hunting of wolves,
are favourites for the Berlin equivalent of Crufts,
the Gold Medal is awarded to one Asmodey.

The shipping tonne is fixed
at 2.8 cubic meters;
transition from paddle wheel to screw propeller;
last days of wooden clippers;
no statistics available
on the Chinese merchantman fleet;
North German Lloyd: 38 vessels, 63,000 tonnes,
Hamburg America Line: 19 vessels, 34,200 tonnes,
Hamburg-Süd: 9 vessels, 13,500 tonnes.

In Baden-Baden Turgenev
pays daily visits to the Viardot sisters,
unforgettable evenings,
his favourite Lied
Schubert's rarely heard
'wenn meine Grillen schwirren',
or they just read aloud from Scheffel's *Ekkehard*.

The following are discovered:
the flightless kiwi-kiwi bird in New Zealand,
the eyeless newt in the limestone caverns at Kranj,
a blind fish in the Mammoth Caves of Kentucky.
The following are investigated:
the erosion of hair covering (whales, dolphins),
the whitening of skin (snails, caddis flies),
formation of body-armour (crabs, insects) –
questions of evolution,
fertility studies,
nature's secrets
lisped back.

Campaign against foreign words,
luna moth, zephyr, chrysalis,
1088 dictionary terms
are to be Germanized.
Shop assistants strike for Sunday afternoons off,
the number of votes polled
by the Social Democrats
in the Berlin election: 68,535.
The Tiergarten ward is free-thinking.
Singer gives his first speech
as a candidate.
13th edition of the Brockhaus
encyclopaedia.

The critics savage Tolstoy's
Power of Darkness,
while Blumenthal's *A Drop of Poison*
is guaranteed a long euphuous run;
'A dark cloud hangs
over the head of Count Albrecht Vahlberg
who occupies a respected place in society
in the capital,'
Zola, Ibsen, Hauptmann
are unwelcome,
Salammbô misconceived,
Liszt cosmopolitan,
and last but not least comes the slot
'The reader writes,'
the explanation of cramp
and the removal of foreign bodies
are what he wants explained to him.

First appearances of:
Pithecanthropus,
Java remnants,
the avatars.
Rendered extinct:
the little Hawaiian fellow
called the sunbird
used in the making of feather coats for the royal family,
a yellow streak of fluff on each wing,

1886 –
birth year of certain Expressionists,
also of State Councillor Furtwängler,
émigré Kokoschka,
General Field Marshall v. W (†),

doubling of equity
at Schneider-Creusot, Putilov, Krupp Steel.

Silence

Silence,
coming from within:
things past,
tender early associations
ended by death;
also days with table-decorations and fruit-bowls
placed between couples
of unwavering commitment, two flames.

Silence,
from faraway estates,
preparations for festivities or homecomings:
beating of carpets,
on which, later,
many pairs of feet will shuffle
in love and dotage.

Silence,
once offered to and endured by strangers,
broken today by a gruff plea:
'stay by me,
maybe not all that much longer,
so much decay in me,
so much heaviness,
fatigue.'

Wet Fences

Wet fences
blown over the land,
dark-green stakes,
murders of crows and shedding poplars
for company.

Wet fences
defining gardens,
though not for descendants
of the renowned tulip Semper Augustus
which in 17th century Paris
changed hands for unheard of sums,
or the hyacinth 'Bleu Passe'
(1600, floruit 1734),
for which you wrote down your name in a book,
and several days later
a head gardener would conduct you past it –
rather for the old and reliable ranunculi of Ostade.

Wet fences,
mouldering and putting on moss
in the silent villages,
little barriers
blown over the land,
but snow collects, and corrosive salts,
dribble of rot –
the old story.

Clemenceau

'With one eye on the end,
life is beautiful'
the eye was on the roses of the Vendée.
Moreover,
'Human beings have no souls,
if only they had a bit of dignity.'

A superior feeling is indicated by the following remark:
'There are stars
that have been extinguished for 2000 years,
and we still see their light.
If you bear that in mind,
everything's OK.'

He knew about art.
On his country neighbour Monet he wrote:
'If he'd been given another ten years to live,
no one would have understood the least bit
of his work,
maybe his canvases would have had
nothing on them at all.'

The following dialogue is amusing:
'C: So, he is said to have been
an enthusiastic pederast?
M: No, he talks about it,
without getting at all excited.
C: What, he didn't even get excited?'

On the subject of our little faible he jested:
'The Germans
see an adorable beast sashaying into the water
and then they call it a sea-pig.'

In place of emphasis, perspective;
aged eighty-five, he offered the following summing-up:
'Nothing is true. Everything is true.
That's the end of wisdom.'

He had been many times to Greece,
had brought home pieces from the Acropolis;
his will ended:
'On my tomb the marble from Hellas.'

Little Sweet Face

Little sweet face,
shrunken already in transit,
snowy-, nearly deathly pale,
great outpouring of grief
when you shortly passed
away –

We played together
quite unmindful of our state of development
all looks back and out
cropped,
living, experiencing nothing
outside the charmed circle
of our own noises!

Hobbled – blinkered! But once,
the men beating the olive-trees, obscured by
    branches,
piles of fruit set to ripen.
Once, wine from the Gulf of Lions
in smoky vaults, accented with sea water.
Or giant eucalypts, 400 feet high,
and the trembling light under their crowns.
Once to Cotroceni –
once only

Little face
snowflake
always so white
and the blue vein at the temple
Ligurian grape-hyacinth
blue,
musk-scented.

How are the beech trees in September

on the Oresund, the Garda of the North,
where as much larkspur flowers
as in the whole of the rest of Europe,
and yonder Sverige,
the proud country.

Poor German sits by the water's edge
if he asks a question in German
the people spit at him,
if he asks it in French
the people don't understand,
and Danish is a difficult language
sweet & soft as whipped cream

Old German
a long time rowing in the galleys,
who-sits-in-galley-
will-see-water-from-below,
incapable of watching the shore
or following the seagulls
all ship's belly
mouldy zwieback
leg-irons,
oil-slick impressions
of the higher life.

Divergences

One says: please no inner life,
manners by all means, but nothing affective,
that's no compensation
for the insufferable
difficulties of outward-directed expression –
those cerebralized
city-Styxes

when my little prince
pokes his chubby little legs through the bars of his
    cot
it melts my heart, it was like that with Otto Ernst,
and it's no different now

the contraries are not easy to reconcile
but when you survey the provinces
the inner life
has it by a neck.

Herr Wehner

This is mine
Herr Wehner
he was our house-tutor
died early of phthisis
once he'd infected my youngest brother
who died of tubercular meningitis.

Came from Lissa
son of a blacksmith
always went around in wooden clogs
which was unusual with us
Liska his bride
stayed with us over Whitsun once
daughter of a police major
ergo different class
the giggling in the evenings
when the mosquitoes buzzed
and it was our bedtime,
but, as I heard later,
it was a rocky marriage.

Herr Wehner,
what makes him mine
is the fact that he is buried somewhere
rotting away in a collective farm in (now) Poland
no one in the village
will remember him
but he sometimes appears to me
grey and isolated
under certain historical aspects.

Little Cultural Commentary

Epochs are slow to change,
Tosca (1902) is still passion,
Bohème (1900) is love,
even from the end of *Twilight of the Gods* (1876)
it's still our ashes that glow.
Some things remain sketchy:
Iphigenia Act v
(at the premiere in 1779, Goethe himself played Orestes):
Thoas's renunciation and humanity
never established themselves
in the political repertoire.

The Ides of March stand in twilight:
if a new form of government is coming,
the old one must make way.
Most people laugh at Leonidas today
(I myself don't).

A barber who delivers a first-class shave
(extremely rare!)
is more remarkable than a court chaplain
(I don't mistake tragedy and the problem of guilt).

And if you're given to talking about existential angst
some Midgard serpent for breakfast,
the illimitable Oceanos in the evening,
and at night the being-thrown-into – then you'll sleep
     soundly –
the West no longer wants to defend itself –
it wants to be scared, it wants that thrown feeling.

A good pop song has more to say about 1950
than 500 pages of cultural crisis.
In the cinema, where you can keep your hat and coat
     with you,
there's more firewater than on the Kothurn,
and without the tedious delays.

(The quaternary was man turned in on himself,
now comes the triploid)
66 chromosomes, giant stature.

And as for the new national anthem!
The words pleasing, perhaps a little insipid,
the logical next step would be
running a bunny skin up the flagpole.

Personally unfruitful,
but I expect it'll happen.

Zeh was a pharmacist,

or claimed to be,
times were tranquil, people didn't ask too many
    questions,
but when a new broom came along, it was duly
    'established that' etc.
and it all contributed to his downfall.

Zeh was an incomparable magician
shelves full of powders & tinctures
not that he had to sell them to you
you were persuaded of their efficacy
in advance.

Zeh had mixed up a slimming-cure
called Zee-an that you hardly even needed to take
it worked in your pocket
you straightaway started to reduce.
He had stuck that preparation
    in one of the pharmacy windows.

Among other things you could see there
herbal teas, pestles & mortars, chatty tips
for di- and nocturnal events of an untoward nature
all of it defying description –
unrivalled in their suggestiveness
from a psychosomatic point of view

his like would never be found again
children (not likely!) *desunt*,
long since turfed out of his grave.

Radio

' – science per se' –
my God, when I hear them on the radio saying that,
it slays me.
Is there a science that's not per se?
I don't get out much, rarely get to see any lakes,
gardens only sporadically and then behind fences,
or in allotments, that's about the size of it,
I rely on ersatz:
radio, newspaper, magazines –
so how can people say such things to me?

It makes you wonder
whether there are any surrogates for hollyhocks,
for warm life, French kisses, hanky-panky,
all those things that make existence a little luxurious,
and all of them somehow of a piece!

No, all this cerebration is not my cup of tea,
but there are sometimes hours on end
where there's no woman on any wavelength
(I receive medium-wave, short-, long-, and VHF),
no voice saying, 'first you say no, then
                                        maybe, then yes',
nothing but these opinionated pedagogues,
it seems that everything the West thinks of as its
higher product is produced by the seated male –
as I say, give me the hanky-panky any day!

' – the last vestiges of the ancient culture would have
    completely disappeared – '
(well, and what if)
' – a sonorous past – '
(la-di-dah)
' – in villages in New Mexico
farmers still bless their fields and livestock
with these songs – '
(very nice, I'm sure,
but I don't get out of Brandenburg much).

We hear Professor Salem Aleikum,
the reporter still slavering over him:
'the professor is lying on the porch of his house
with his lute cradled in his arm
singing the old ballads' –
probably on an ottoman,
with a carafe of ice water at his side,
rejecting old hypotheses, putting out new ones –

the great rivers of the world
the Nile, the Brahmaputra, or what the hell do I know
wouldn't be enough to drown all those professors –

don't have any acreage, don't have any livestock,
nothing blesses me, life is one continuous affliction,
but nothing like those professors
teach, teach, teach,
from every pore,
who turn everything into illustrated lecture (with slides).

Thinking

Thinking –
has a reach of about four feet,
it can just about cope with one load of information at a time
but other than that?

Take sheep-herding,
an entire continent lives by it,
then along come synthetic fibres
and the mouflons are *foutus*.
Cause: anti-social inventors,
obsessive test tube johnnies –
nature's waifs and strays.

Or science
one-track, purposive,
woven from Anglo-Saxon material.

Or take the essay world,
one man stitches up another
while the rest of the brotherhood look on.

'It's simply not possible to take you seriously any more' –
gawdhelpus – priceless knockabout!

But there's one thought that is the reality of the gods,
its wellspring may indeed be murky,
but then it's there
full of memory of her

who shall remain nameless.

Breathe

Irritability, grief
positively fur-lined
and then you'll see:

'Knock back
a couple of shorts
good and cold
and clear
then raise your beer glass
steady eye
foam-born
intact
unalloyed
no half-measures
or additives
pure yard-arm
humming along
gruff (but when not)
teeth well-cemented
no sweat or BO
dry-backed

prime of life
flesh that will make it through the night
sleep-garlanded
richly festooned'

Now take a breath.

Till the onset of more losses
griefs
irritabilities
positively fur-lined.

Listen

Listen, this is what the last evening will be like
when you're still capable of going out: you're smoking your
    Junos,
quaffing your three pints of Würzburger Hofbräu
and reading about the UN as reflected in the pages of the
    Spiegel,

you're sitting alone at your little table, the least possible
    company
beside the radiator, because you crave warmth.
All round you mankind and its mewling,
the married couple and their loathsome hound.

That's all you are, you've no house or hill
to call your own, to dream in a sunny landscape,
from your birth to this evening
the walls around you were always pretty tightly drawn.

That's all you were, but Zeus and all the immortals,
the great souls, the cosmos and all the suns
were there for you too, spun and fed through you,
that's all you were, finished as begun –
your last evening – good night.

Fragments 1953

A day without tears is a rare occurrence
                    culpable absent-mindedness
practically an episode

                              *

when men still wore starched collars,
and stuffed cotton wool between their toes
hobbled about in pain, pedicure hadn't been invented,
but you would see faces that were worth a second look
those were years when something whispered

Fragments 1955

30x endured agonies at the dentist's
100x treated myself to expensive imported roses
4x shed tears beside open graves
left 25 women
2x had a pocket full of money and 98x not,
at the end of the day you take out an insurance policy
at 12.50 per month,
to be certain of being buried

*

Or those 3 bars of Tchaikovsky
that you recognize 3 floors away

*

what are you? A symptom,
an ape, a gnome –

nestling in the summer,
the freshness of   & forest –